If you have a home computer with Internet access you may:

- request an item to be placed on hold.

- renew an item that is not overdue or on hold.

- view titles and due dates checked out on your card.

- view and/or pay your outstanding fines online (over $5).

To view your patron record from your home computer click on Patchogue-Medford Library's homepage: **www.pmlib.org**

THE FLORIDA MARLINS

BY

MARK STEWART

Content Consultant
James L. Gates, Jr.
Library Director
National Baseball Hall of Fame and Museum

NORWOODHOUSE PRESS

CHICAGO, ILLINOIS

Norwood House Press
P.O. Box 316598
Chicago, Illinois 60631

For information regarding Norwood House Press, please visit our website at:
www.norwoodhousepress.com or call 866-565-2900.

All photos courtesy of Getty Images except the following:
Black Book archives (6, 21 top, 41 top right & bottom left);
Topps, Inc. (7, 14, 20, 21 bottom, 22, 23, 36, 38, 40 top & bottom left, 43).
Cover photo by Doug Benc/Getty Images.
Special thanks to Topps, Inc.

Editor: Mike Kennedy
Designer: Ron Jaffe
Project Management: Black Book Partners, LLC.
Special thanks to Darryl Laird.

Library of Congress Cataloging-in-Publication Data

Stewart, Mark, 1960-
   The Florida Marlins / by Mark Stewart ; content consultant, James L.
Gates, Jr.
      p. cm. -- (Team spirit)
   Summary: "Presents the history, accomplishments and key personalities
of the Florida Marlins baseball team. Includes timelines, quotes, maps,
glossary and website"--Provided by publisher.
   Includes bibliographical references and index.
   ISBN-13: 978-1-59953-167-0 (library edition : alk. paper)
   ISBN-10: 1-59953-167-4 (library edition : alk. paper) 1. Florida Marlins
(Baseball team)--History--Juvenile literature. I. Gates, James L. II.
Title.
GV956.F56S74 2008
796.357'6409759381--dc22

                                             2007043497

COVER PHOTO: The Marlins celebrate a victory during the 2007 season.

Table of Contents

SPORTS WORDS & VOCABULARY WORDS: In this book, you will find many words that are new to you. You may also see familiar words used in new ways. The glossary on page 46 gives the meanings of baseball words, as well as "everyday" words that have special baseball meanings. These words appear in **bold type** throughout the book. The glossary on page 47 gives the meanings of vocabulary words that are not related to baseball. They appear in ***bold italic type*** throughout the book.

Meet the Marlins

There are many ways to build a winning team in baseball. Some teams bring their young players along slowly and then add older players when the time is right. The mix of youth and experience helps the club during a long season. On the other hand, some teams put their **prospects** on the field and just say, "Go get 'em!"

The Florida Marlins have found success both ways. They won their first **World Series** with many well-known stars. They won their second World Series with players many fans had never heard of!

This book tells the story of the Marlins. They love baseball and live to play the game. The Marlins are a team that is always focused on winning. But they are also willing to be *patient* in seasons when the team struggles because of injuries and inexperience. The question for many Marlins fans is not *What will they do next?* It is usually *How will they win next?*

The Marlins gather at home plate to celebrate a win in 2007.

Way Back When

When the **National League (NL)** decided to add two new teams for the 1993 season, everyone in baseball knew that one of those teams would almost certainly be located in Florida. But which city? Groups from Orlando, Miami, and the Tampa Bay area all gave great reasons why they should get a club. The final choice was Miami.

H. Wayne Huizenga, the owner of the team, wanted to attract fans from all over the state. That is why he chose to name the club the Florida Marlins. That way, everyone in the region felt like the team was theirs.

The Marlins struggled in their early seasons even though they had some good players. Jeff Conine, Gary Sheffield, Charles Johnson, and Robb Nen were the team's first stars. In 1996, Kevin Brown, Al Leiter, and Devon White joined the club. A year later, the Marlins added

Moises Alou, Alex Fernandez, and Bobby Bonilla.

At the same time, young players such as Edgar Renteria, Luis Castillo, Craig Counsell, and Livan Hernandez began to contribute. The Marlins went from having a losing record in their first four seasons to winning the World Series in 1997. They beat the Cleveland Indians in one of the most thrilling finishes ever.

After the World Series, Huizenga broke up the team by trading away many of his best —and highest paid—players. The fans were unhappy with those moves. Many stayed away from the ballpark. In 1999, Huizenga decided he would rather be a baseball fan than a team owner, and he sold the Marlins to businessman John Henry.

Florida soon dropped in the **standings**. From 1998 to 2002, the team had a losing record every year. However, the Marlins slowly rebuilt their roster with exciting young players. They had a group of hard-throwing pitchers, including Brad Penny, A.J. Burnett, Carl Pavano, Josh Beckett, and Braden Looper. They also had some very

LEFT: Moises Alou, a star on the 1997 Marlins.
ABOVE: Josh Beckett, who helped Florida return to the top of baseball.

good hitters, including Derrek Lee, Mike Lowell, and Juan Pierre.

In 2003, the team signed **All-Star** catcher Ivan Rodriguez to handle the young **pitching staff**. The Marlins also promoted Miguel Cabrera and Dontrelle Willis to the **major leagues**. Those three players gave Florida a spark. After starting the year slowly, the Marlins finished strong and made the **playoffs** as the NL **Wild Card**. Against all odds, they won the **pennant** and beat the powerful New York Yankees in the World Series.

Amazing as it may seem, the Marlins had just two winning seasons in their first 11 years. Yet both times they ended up as champions of baseball. The experts learned one important lesson from Florida's formula for success—if you combine the right players and the right team chemistry at just the right time, great things can happen. The Marlins have two World Series titles to prove it.

LEFT: Miguel Cabrera, one of the young stars who led the Marlins to the championship in 2003.   **ABOVE**: Dontrelle Willis fires a pitch for Florida.

The Team Today

A marlin is a swift, powerful fish that moves through the water with great confidence. That is also a good way to describe the team—though these Marlins play on grass, of course. Even in years when Florida does not have a winning record, the players never give up and never give in. Their fans know a lot about baseball, and they cheer their team for a strong effort.

The Marlins have always focused on developing young players. Some are *scouted* and signed by the club. Others come to Florida in trades with other teams. The Marlins are very good at finding young talent, and they are not afraid to take a risk on a player another team has given up on.

In recent years, exciting stars such as Jeremy Hermida, Josh Willingham, Hanley Ramirez, Dan Uggla, and Mike Jacobs have joined the Marlins. They learned from Dontrelle Willis and Miguel Cabrera, who played for the team when it won a championship in 2003. The Marlins hope to hit on the right mix of players to lift them to another World Series.

Dan Uggla and Hanley Ramirez walk out to their positions in the field.

Home Turf

The Marlins play in a stadium located in Miami Gardens, a town just north of the city of Miami. The stadium was built for the Miami Dolphins football team in 1987, but the field was made extra-wide to fit baseball and soccer games as well. Before the Marlins moved to their stadium in 1993, 660 new lights had to be added for night baseball.

The Marlins' ballpark has one of the deepest outfields in baseball. It is very hard to hit home runs, especially to center field. The park has other interesting features, including a pitcher's mound that can be lowered underground when the Dolphins want to take the field. The stadium also has an underground drainage system that can get the field in playing shape 30 minutes after a rainstorm.

BY THE NUMBERS

- *The Marlins' stadium has 42,531 seats for baseball.*
- *The distance from home plate to the left field foul pole is 330 feet.*
- *The distance from home plate to the center field fence is 404 feet.*
- *The distance from home plate to the right field foul pole is 345 feet.*
- *There have been four Super Bowls played in the stadium, and a fifth one is scheduled for 2010.*

The Atlanta Braves and the Marlins line up on Florida's home field before Opening Day in 2005.

Dressed for Success

Since the Marlins started playing in 1993, they have used a combination of teal and black as their team colors. Teal, which mixes green and blue, reminds many people of ocean water. It is a perfect choice for a team called the Marlins.

In their early years, the Marlins wore teal hats and featured the color throughout their uniform. They even had a sleeveless jersey, and the t-shirt they slipped on underneath their top was teal. The large scoreboard in left field is called the "Teal Monster." Fans sometimes shout "Feel the Teal!" when the Marlins are beating an opponent. Recently, Florida switched to black as its primary color. The team also has a pinstripe uniform style.

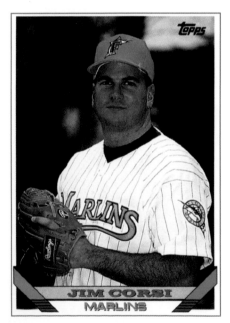

Florida's *logo* has always included a picture of a marlin. It also spells out the team's entire name. The Marlins are one of just five NL teams with a logo done in that style.

Jim Corsi models the pinstripe uniform the Marlins wore in their early years.

UNIFORM BASICS

The baseball uniform has not changed much since the Marlins began playing. It has four main parts:

- a cap or batting helmet with a sun visor
- a top with a player's number on the back
- pants that reach down between the ankle and the knee
- stirrup-style socks

The uniform top sometimes has a player's name on the back. The team's name, city, or logo is usually on the front. Baseball teams wear light-colored uniforms when they play at home and darker styles when they play on the road.

For more than 100 years, baseball uniforms were made of wool *flannel* and were very baggy. This helped the sweat *evaporate* and gave players the freedom to move around. Today's uniforms are made of *synthetic* fabrics that stretch with players and keep them dry and cool.

Josh Willingham wears one of Florida's 2007 home uniforms.

We Won!

During their first 11 seasons, the Marlins had a winning record only twice. In those two years, they were not just good—they were great! Each time, Florida found the perfect mix of pitching, hitting, and defense to win the World Series.

No one paid much attention to the Marlins during the 1997 season. The team finished far behind the Atlanta Braves in the **NL East**. Florida made it to the playoffs as a Wild Card thanks to *experienced* players such as Kevin Brown, Al Leiter, Gary Sheffield, Jeff Conine, Devon White, Bobby Bonilla, Darren Daulton, and Moises Alou. They were joined by young stars Edgar Renteria, Charles Johnson, Robb Nen, Alex Fernandez, and Livan Hernandez.

Despite the odds against his team, manager Jim Leyland got the Marlins believing they could do anything. In any game, any player felt like he could be a hero. In the first round of the playoffs, Florida swept the San Francisco

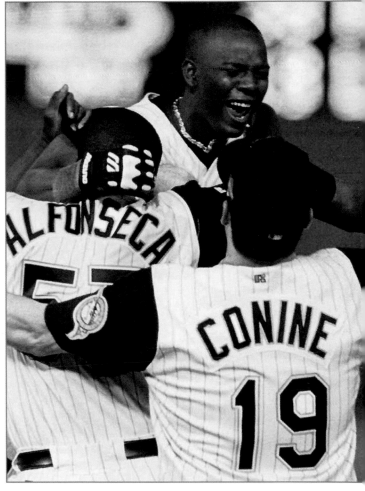

LEFT: Livan Hernandez and Jim Leyland
RIGHT: Teammates mob Edgar Renteria after his hit that won the 1997 World Series.

Giants in three games. Against the Braves in the **National League Championship Series (NLCS)**, Brown and Hernandez won two games each. The Marlins batted just .199 as a team, but they got **clutch hits** when they needed them. Hernandez struck out 15 Braves in Game Five and was named the **Most Valuable Player (MVP)** of the series.

Florida faced the Cleveland Indians in the 1997 World Series. Both teams hit well, and the series seesawed back and forth. In the exciting seventh game, the Indians led 2–1 in the bottom of the ninth inning. Craig Counsell, who was playing in place of injured Luis Castillo, tied the game. Two innings later, Counsell was standing on third base with two outs. Renteria, Florida's youngest player, drove him home with a single to center field. The Marlins were champions!

Six years later, the Marlins were up to their old tricks. Once again, the Braves had a big lead in the NL East, and once again the Marlins played just well enough to make the playoffs as a Wild Card. Florida was a very young team. Catcher Ivan Rodriguez was the only everyday player over the age of 30.

As in 1997, the 2003 Marlins seemed to have a new hero every day. Derrek Lee, Miguel Cabrera, and Mike Lowell supplied power. Juan Pierre and Luis Castillo gave the team great speed. Josh Beckett, Dontrelle Willis, Brad Penny, and Carl Pavano **anchored** a good pitching staff. Manager Jack McKeon seemed never to make a wrong decision.

The Marlins beat the Giants and the Chicago Cubs in the playoffs to win the pennant. They were behind in both series, but each time they found a way to win. Against the Cubs in the NLCS,

ABOVE: Brad Penny throws a pitch during the 2003 World Series.
RIGHT: Mike Lowell watches as Alex Gonzalez, Ivan Rodriguez, and Derrek Lee celebrate Florida's second championship.

Florida was just two innings away from losing. The Marlins scored eight runs in the eighth inning to win Game Six and pounded Chicago's pitching in Game Seven for two **remarkable** victories.

In the World Series, Pierre's speed helped the Marlins beat the New York Yankees in Game One. After losing the next two games, Florida tied the series when shortstop Alex Gonzalez hit a home run in the bottom of the 12th inning of Game Four.

The Marlins won Game Five and then sent 23-year-old Beckett to the mound for Game Six. Though he had pitched against

the Yankees just three days earlier, he was ready to face the Bronx Bombers again. In one of the greatest pitching performances ever, Beckett **overpowered** the Yankees for nine innings and won the game 2–0. The Marlins were champions again!

Go-To Guys

To be a true star in baseball, you need more than a quick bat and a strong arm. You have to be a "go-to guy"—someone the manager wants on the pitcher's mound or in the batter's box when it matters most. Fans of the Marlins have had a lot to cheer about over the years, including these great stars …

THE PIONEERS

JEFF CONINE   Outfielder/First Baseman

- BORN: 6/27/1966   • PLAYED FOR TEAM: 1993 TO 1997 & 2003 TO 2005

JEFF CONINE
MARLINS

Jeff Conine was the Marlins' most dependable player in their early years. He was a good hitter and leader who came to the ballpark ready to play every day.

ROBB NEN   Pitcher

- BORN: 11/28/1969
- PLAYED FOR TEAM: 1993 TO 1997

With Robb Nen on the mound at the end of a game, the Marlins knew they had a great chance to win. During his years in Florida, he was one of the best **closers** in baseball.

GARY SHEFFIELD   Outfielder

- BORN: 11/18/1968
- PLAYED FOR TEAM: 1993 TO 1998

Gary Sheffield was an infielder before he joined the Marlins. The team needed a **slugger** in the outfield, and he agreed to move to a new position. In 1996, Sheffield hit 42 home runs and drove in 120 runs.

CHARLES JOHNSON   Catcher

- BORN: 7/20/1971
- PLAYED FOR TEAM: 1994 TO 1998 & 2001 TO 2002

Charles Johnson was the NL's best defensive catcher in the mid-1990s. He won a **Gold Glove** with the Marlins three times.

LUIS CASTILLO   Second Baseman

- BORN: 9/12/1975
- PLAYED FOR TEAM: 1996 TO 2005

Luis Castillo was one of the fastest players in baseball when he played for the Marlins. He led the NL in stolen bases twice.

LEFT: Jeff Conine
TOP RIGHT: Gary Sheffield
BOTTOM RIGHT: Luis Castillo

MIKE LOWELL   Third Baseman

• BORN: 2/24/1974   • PLAYED FOR TEAM: 1999 TO 2005

Mike Lowell was traded to the Marlins by the Yankees. In 2003, he led Florida with 32 home runs and 105 **runs batted in (RBI)**. Lowell then helped Florida beat New York in the World Series.

JOSH BECKETT   Pitcher

• BORN: 5/15/1980   • PLAYED FOR TEAM: 2001 TO 2005

Josh Beckett grew up in Texas *idolizing* superstars Nolan Ryan and Roger Clemens, who were also Texans. In 2003, Beckett did something that neither of his idols had done—he pitched a **shutout** to win the World Series.

DONTRELLE WILLIS   Pitcher

• BORN: 1/12/1982   • PLAYED FOR TEAM: 2003 TO 2007

When Dontrelle Willis joined the Marlins, fans all over the country fell in love with him and jammed into ballparks whenever he pitched. Willis had an unusual pitching style, a great attitude, and an amazing fastball.

TOP LEFT: Mike Lowell   **TOP RIGHT**: Miguel Cabrera
BOTTOM LEFT: Dontrelle Willis   **BOTTOM RIGHT**: Hanley Ramirez

MIGUEL CABRERA · Third Baseman/Outfielder

- BORN: 4/18/1983
- PLAYED FOR TEAM: 2003 TO 2007

Miguel Cabrera had just turned 20 when the Marlins made him an everyday player in 2003. He brought with him his joy for the game and a powerful bat. A few months after Cabrera joined the club, the Marlins won the World Series.

DAN UGGLA · Second Baseman

- BORN: 3/11/1980   • FIRST YEAR WITH TEAM: 2006

Second basemen are normally good fielders and fast runners who hit with little power. Dan Uggla gave the Marlins muscle at the position. In his first two season, he hit 58 homers and drove in 178 runs.

HANLEY RAMIREZ · Shortstop

- BORN: 12/23/1983   • FIRST YEAR WITH TEAM: 2006

The Marlins were not happy to trade Josh Beckett to the Boston Red Sox after the 2005 season, but they could not pass up the chance to get Hanley Ramirez. The exciting young shortstop quickly became one of the NL's best **all-around** players.

On the Sidelines

During their brief history, the Marlins have had some excellent baseball men in their dugout. Their first manager, Rene Lachemann, had been a coach for four pennant-winning teams in the **American League (AL)**. He taught the Marlins the *fundamentals* of baseball. John Boles followed Lachemann and took two turns managing the team. He helped the Marlins become a more hardworking club.

The manager who brought Florida its first championship was Jim Leyland. He was very good at mixing the talents of his players. They respected Leyland and played hard for him. The same was true of Jack McKeon, who managed the team to its 2003 title. Though McKeon was in his seventies, he did a great job with Florida's young players. Joe Girardi took over for McKeon and was named NL Manager of the Year.

In 2007, Fredi Gonzalez was hired to manage the Marlins. Like many of the **skippers** he followed, Gonzalez had a fine record as a coach. He worked in that role with both the Marlins and the Atlanta Braves.

Jim Leyland waves a championship flag after Florida's 1997 World Series title.

One Great Day

The 2003 World Series was supposed to be an easy one for the mighty New York Yankees. They had won 101 games during the season and had just defeated the Boston Red Sox in a thrilling playoff series. The Marlins, on the other hand, were young and inexperienced. What chance did they have?

The series was tied 1–1 when Josh Beckett faced Mike Mussina in Game Three. Beckett was very talented, but he was also *injury-prone*. During the 2003 season, he hurt his elbow and won just nine games. Against the Yankees, however, he pitched very well. Though Beckett lost Game Three, manager Jack McKeon saw how the New York hitters struggled to hit his fastball.

Four days later, the Marlins took the field against the Yankees in New York, leading the series three games to two. McKeon surprised everyone when he announced that Beckett would be his **starting pitcher**. With only three days of rest, Beckett might not have the

energy he needed to handle the New York hitters again.

When the game began, the fans at Yankee Stadium were noisy. They were expecting a victory. Beckett quieted them by striking out the first batter he faced, Derek Jeter. Inning after inning, he burned his fastball over the plate, and the New York hitters could not catch up to it.

Andy Pettitte was almost as good for the Yankees, but the Marlins scored two runs against him. That was all Beckett needed. He seemed to get stronger—not weaker—as the game wore on. Amazingly, he gave up only five hits and struck out nine Yankees.

With two outs in the bottom of the ninth, Beckett fired a pitch to Jorge Posada, who hit a slow roller toward first base. Beckett raced off the mound, gloved the grounder, and tagged Posada for the final out. The Marlins won 2–0 and were champions of baseball.

Legend Has It

Why did Josh Beckett wear number 61 when he joined the Marlins?

LEGEND HAS IT that he wanted number 19. Beckett had worn that number in high school and in the **minor leagues**. Baseball players are very *superstitious*, and he wanted to keep his "lucky" number when he was promoted to the big leagues. The problem was that an older player, Mike Lowell, already wore number 19 for the Marlins. Beckett simply turned number 19 upside down and chose number 61.

ABOVE: Josh Beckett wears #61.   **RIGHT**: Dontrelle Willis's mom throws out the first pitch before a Little League World Series game.

Which Marlin was closest to his mother?

LEGEND HAS IT that Dontrelle Willis was. His mom, Joyce, was a catcher in a fast-pitch softball league when she was pregnant with him. After he was born, she taught him everything he knew about pitching. Each year he played for the Marlins, Willis wrote his mom's name under the bill of his cap.

Which Marlin had the best collection of bobblehead dolls?

LEGEND HAS IT that Miguel Cabrera did. He had old bobbleheads and new ones, and bobbleheads of many of his former Florida teammates. His most prized bobbleheads were the 1997 versions of Jeff Conine and Craig Counsell. Cabrera got them as a fan when he went to a Marlins game.

It Really Happened

When a team begins a season by losing 22 of its first 38 games, the fans can usually expect a long, disappointing summer. Florida fans felt this way in 2003. The Marlins had one of the worst records in baseball. The team hoped to change its luck by replacing manager Jeff Torborg with Jack McKeon.

McKeon had been managing since the 1970s. He was known for keeping his team relaxed and giving young players a chance to learn and mature. He also was not afraid to make big changes. In that lost season of 2003, McKeon seemed like the perfect man to help the young Marlins improve.

What happened next still has baseball people shaking their heads. McKeon handed the ball to his young pitchers—Dontrelle Willis, Brad Penny, Carl Pavano, Mark Redman, and Josh Beckett—and told them to go have some fun. He also called up Miguel Cabrera from the minors to be his left fielder. Just 20 years old, Cabrera had been a third baseman.

Every one of McKeon's moves seemed to work. Cabrera hit a homer in his first game for the Marlins. Willis, who joined the team in May, found himself on the All-Star team in July!

Jack McKeon celebrates with his team in 2003.

The Marlins started winning, and soon they set their sights on the playoffs. Florida piled up 18 victories in September—including wins in six of their last seven games—to earn the NL Wild Card. It was an absolutely amazing *comeback*. Under McKeon, the Marlins went 75–49.

In the playoffs, Florida surprised the San Francisco Giants and Chicago Cubs. The Marlins next defeated the mighty New York Yankees in the World Series. When the Manager of the Year award was announced that winter, no one was surprised—McKeon was the winner.

Team Spirit

Marlins fans come in all shapes and sizes. Many people from around the United States move to Florida when they retire. The state also attracts a lot of young people. Millions of Spanish-speaking Americans make their home there, too. That is why the crowds at Marlins games are different depending on the day of the week and the time of the game. The fans all have one thing in common—they love baseball.

The most loyal Marlins fans support the team through its ups and downs. They squeeze into the stadium when the team makes it to the playoffs and World Series. They also buy tickets when the team is rebuilding. They know that the young players learning the game may soon lead the Marlins to glory again.

The fans also enjoy the performance of Billy the Marlin, the team's *mascot.* He is one of the most popular characters in baseball. Billy has arms and legs, and wears the head of a marlin. He was supposed to make his first appearance on Opening Day in 1997, but the man who played Billy lost the top of his costume. To this day, fans love to shout, "Bring me the head of Billy the Marlin!"

Florida fans count the number of strikeouts recorded by the Marlins' pitching staff during a playoff game in 1997.

Timeline

Luis Castillo and Edgar Renteria turn a double play.

1993
The Marlins finish their first season with a record of 64–98.

1996
Luis Castillo and Edgar Renteria—both 20— are baseball's youngest double play duo.

1995
Quilvio Veras leads the NL in stolen bases.

1997
The Marlins win their first World Series.

2001
A.J. Burnett pitches a **no-hitter** against the San Diego Padres.

Quilvio Veras

A.J. Burnett

Hanley
Ramirez

2003
The Marlins win their
second World Series.

2007
Hanley Ramirez has the highest
slugging average of any shortstop.

2002
Luis Castillo
has a 35-game
hitting streak.

2005
Jeremy Hermida hits a
pinch-hit grand slam in his
first **at-bat** as a major leaguer.

2006
Anibal Sanchez
pitches a no-hitter.

Jeremy
Hermida

Anibal Sanchez
after his no-hitter.

Fun Facts

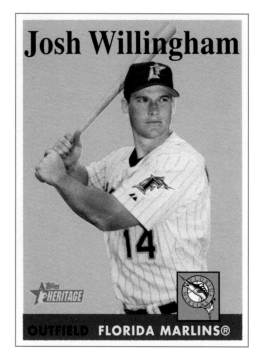

Josh Willingham

OUTFIELD FLORIDA MARLINS®

BIG FOUR

The 2006 Marlins had four **rookie** pitchers who won 10 or more games—Anibal Sanchez, Ricky Nolasco, Josh Johnson, and Scott Olsen. No team had ever done that before.

BIG THREE

The 2006 Marlins also had three rookies who hit 20 or more home runs—Dan Uggla, Josh Willingham, and Mike Jacobs. No team had ever done that before, either!

WIN WHEN IT COUNTS

In their first 15 seasons, the Marlins never won a division title. However, they did make the playoffs twice as a Wild Card and never lost a postseason series.

ABOVE: Josh Willingham   **RIGHT**: Charles Johnson and Kevin Brown meet on the mound during the 1997 playoffs.

WILD MAN

When A.J. Burnett pitched a no-hitter against the San Diego Padres in 2001, he walked nine batters. It was the most walks ever allowed by a pitcher during a no-hitter.

MR. PERFECT

In 1997, catcher Charles Johnson set a record by making no errors in 973 fielding chances.

HELP ME OUT!

In 1996, Kevin Brown won 17 games and lost 11. The team scored a total of just 11 runs in those losses.

MIGHTY MIGGY

Miguel Cabrera hit a game-winning home run in his first game as a Marlin. Only two other players in history—Josh Bard in 2002 and Billy Parker in 1971—had done that before.

Talking Baseball

"I've been playing baseball since I was four. I've got baseball in my blood. I love baseball."

—*Hanley Ramirez, on his passion for the game*

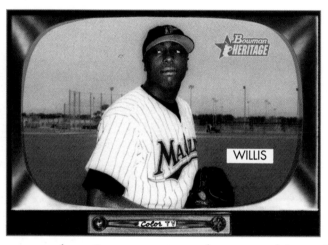

"How can I feel pressure doing what I love to do?"

—*Miguel Cabrera, on staying relaxed during games*

"I want to make guys put the ball in play. If I give up ten hits, then I give up ten hits— but I want to work on making them earn it."

—*Dontrelle Willis, on the secret of pitching*

"You've got to have some arrogant bones in your body, especially to be a pitcher in the big leagues."

—*Josh Beckett, on why it's good to think of yourself as one of the best*

"Play as hard as you can, and when things get tough, just work harder to get better."

—Gary Sheffield, on playing and practicing

"Growing up, you're in the backyard and every time you're playing you're imagining you're in the World Series—Game Seven, 3–2 count. And then you're actually out there in Yankee Stadium trying to win it. It's amazing!"

—Derek Lee, on playing the New York Yankees in the 2003 World Series

"If your style gets production, keep your style. If it doesn't, you might want to change your style … I want results. I don't care how you do it."

—Jim Leyland, on what he expects from his players

LEFT: Dontrelle Willis
ABOVE: Jim Leyland

For the Record

The great Marlins teams and players have left their marks on the record books. These are the "best of the best" …

MARLINS AWARD WINNERS

WINNER	AWARD	YEAR
Livan Hernandez	NLCS MVP	1997
Livan Hernandez	World Series MVP	1997
Jack McKeon	Manager of the Year	2003
Dontrelle Willis	Rookie of the Year*	2003
Ivan Rodriguez	NLCS MVP	2003
Josh Beckett	World Series MVP	2003
Hanley Ramirez	Rookie of the Year	2006
Joe Girardi	Manager of the Year	2006

* The annual award given to each league's best first-year player.

Josh Beckett

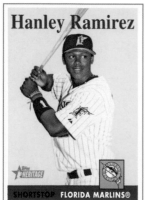

Hanley Ramirez

Livan Hernandez

MARLINS ACHIEVEMENTS

ACHIEVEMENT	YEAR
NL Wild Card	1997
NL Pennant Winners	1997
World Series Champions	1997
NL Wild Card	2003
NL Pennant Winners	2003
World Series Champions	2003

Moises Alou (**LEFT**), Kevin Brown (**TOP**), and Bobby Bonilla (**ABOVE**), key members of the 1997 champs.

41

Pinpoints

The history of a baseball team is made up of many smaller stories. These stories take place all over the map—not just in the city a team calls "home." Match the pushpins on these maps to the Team Facts and you will begin to see the story of the Marlins unfold!

TEAM FACTS

1 Miami Gardens, Florida—*The team has played here since 1993.*

2 Oakland, California—*Dontrelle Willis was born here.*

3 Spring, Texas—*Josh Beckett was born here.*

4 Tampa, Florida—*Gary Sheffield was born here.*

5 Tacoma, Washington—*Jeff Conine was born here.*

6 Blackwell, Oklahoma—*Brad Penny was born here.*

7 Mobile, Alabama—*Juan Pierre was born here.*

8 South Amboy, New Jersey—*Jack McKeon was born here.*

9 North Little Rock, Arkansas—*A.J. Burnett was born here.*

10 San Pedro de Macoris, Dominican Republic—*Luis Castillo was born here.*

11 San Juan, Puerto Rico—*Mike Lowell was born here.*

12 Maracay, Venezuela—*Miguel Cabrera was born here.*

Juan Pierre

Play Ball

Baseball is a game played between two teams over nine innings. Teams take one turn at bat and one turn in the field during each inning. A turn at bat ends when three outs are made. The batters on the hitting team try to reach base safely. The players on the fielding team try to prevent this from happening.

In baseball, the ball is controlled by the pitcher. The pitcher must throw the ball to the batter, who decides whether or not to swing at each pitch. If a batter swings and misses, it is a strike. If the batter lets a good pitch go by, it is also a strike. If the batter swings and the ball does not stay in fair territory (between the v-shaped lines that begin at home plate) it is called "foul," and is counted as a strike. If the pitcher throws three strikes, the batter is out. If the pitcher throws four bad pitches before that, the batter is awarded first base. This is called a base-on-balls, or "walk."

When the batter swings the bat and hits the ball, everyone springs into action. If a fielder catches a batted ball before it hits the ground, the batter is out. If a fielder scoops the ball off the ground and throws it to first base before the batter arrives, the batter is out. If the batter reaches first base safely, he is credited with a hit. A one-base hit is called a single, a two-base hit is called a double, a three-base hit is called a triple, and a four-base hit is called a home run.

Runners who reach base are only safe when they are touching one of the bases. If they are caught between the bases, the fielders can tag them with the ball and record an out.

A batter who is able to circle the bases and make it back to home plate before three outs are made is credited with a run scored. The team with the most runs after nine innings is the winner.

Anyone who has played baseball (or softball) knows that it can be a complicated game. Every player on the field has a job to do. Different players have different strengths and weaknesses. The pitchers, batters, and managers make hundreds of decisions every game. The more you play and watch baseball, the more "little things" you are likely to notice. The next time you are at a game, look for these plays:

PLAY LIST

DOUBLE PLAY—A play where the fielding team is able to make two outs on one batted ball. This usually happens when a runner is on first base, and the batter hits a ground ball to one of the infielders. The base runner is forced out at second base and the ball is then thrown to first base before the batter arrives.

HIT AND RUN—A play where the runner on first base sprints to second base while the pitcher is throwing the ball to the batter. When the second baseman or shortstop moves toward the base to wait for the catcher's throw, the batter tries to hit the ball to the place that the fielder has just left. If the batter swings and misses, the fielding team can tag the runner out.

INTENTIONAL WALK—A play when the pitcher throws four bad pitches on purpose, allowing the batter to walk to first base. This happens when the pitcher would much rather face the next batter—and is willing to risk putting a runner on base.

SACRIFICE BUNT—A play where the batter makes an out on purpose so that a teammate can move to the next base. On a bunt, the batter tries to "deaden" the pitch with the bat instead of swinging at it.

SHOESTRING CATCH—A play where an outfielder catches a short hit an inch or two above the ground, near the tops of his shoes. It is not easy to run as fast as you can and lower your glove without slowing down. It can be risky, too. If a fielder misses a shoestring catch, the ball might roll all the way to the fence.

Glossary

BASEBALL WORDS TO KNOW

ALL-AROUND—Good at all parts of the game.

ALL-STAR—A player who is selected to play in baseball's annual All-Star Game.

AMERICAN LEAGUE (AL)—One of baseball's two major leagues; the AL began play in 1901.

AT-BAT—A turn hitting.

CLOSERS—Relief pitchers who finish close games.

CLUTCH HITS—Hits made under great pressure.

GOLD GLOVE—An award given each year to baseball's best fielders.

GRAND SLAM—A home run with the bases loaded.

MAJOR LEAGUES—The top level of professional baseball leagues.

MINOR LEAGUES—The many professional leagues that help develop players for the major leagues.

MOST VALUABLE PLAYER (MVP)—An award given each year to each league's top player; an MVP is also selected for the World Series and All-Star Game.

NATIONAL LEAGUE (NL)—The older of the two major leagues; the NL began play in 1876.

NATIONAL LEAGUE CHAMPIONSHIP SERIES (NLCS)—The competition that has decided the National League pennant since 1969.

NL EAST—A group of National League teams that plays in the eastern part of the country.

NO-HITTER—A game in which a team is unable to get a hit.

PENNANT—A league championship. The term comes from the triangular flag awarded to each season's champion, beginning in the 1870s.

PINCH-HIT—Taking a teammate's turn to hit.

PITCHING STAFF—The group of players who pitch for a team.

PLAYOFFS—The games played after the regular season to determine which teams will advance to the World Series.

PROSPECTS—Young players who are expected to become stars.

ROOKIE—A player in his first season.

RUNS BATTED IN (RBI)—A statistic that counts the number of runners a batter drives home.

SHUTOUT—A game in which one team does not allow its opponent to score a run.

SKIPPERS—Another term for managers.

SLUGGER—A powerful hitter.

SLUGGING AVERAGE—A statistic that helps measure a hitter's power. It is calculated by dividing the number of total bases a batter has by his official times at bat.

STANDINGS—A daily list of teams, starting with the team with the best record and ending with the team with the worst record.

STARTING PITCHER—The pitcher who begins the game for his team.

WILD CARD—A playoff spot reserved for the team with the best record that has not won its division.

WORLD SERIES—The world championship series played between the winners of the National League and American League.

OTHER WORDS TO KNOW

ANCHORED—Held steady.

COMEBACK—The process of catching up from behind, or making up a large deficit.

EVAPORATE—Disappear, or turn into vapor.

EXPERIENCED—Having knowledge and skill in a job.

FLANNEL—A soft wool or cotton material.

FUNDAMENTALS—The most basic parts of something.

IDOLIZING—Admiring greatly.

INJURY-PRONE—Likely to get hurt.

LOGO—A symbol or design that represents a company or team.

MASCOT—An animal or person believed to bring a group good luck.

OVERPOWERED—Taken control of with force.

PATIENT—Able to wait calmly.

REMARKABLE—Unusual or exceptional.

SCOUTED—Watched closely.

SUPERSTITIOUS—Trusting in magic or luck.

SYNTHETIC—Made in a laboratory, not in nature.

Places to Go

ON THE ROAD

FLORIDA MARLINS
2269 Dan Marino Boulevard
Miami, Florida   33056
(305) 350-5050

NATIONAL BASEBALL HALL OF FAME AND MUSEUM
25 Main Street
Cooperstown, New York   13326
(888) 425-5633
www.baseballhalloffame.org

ON THE WEB

THE FLORIDA MARLINS   www.marlins.com
 • *Learn more about the Marlins*

MAJOR LEAGUE BASEBALL   www.mlb.com
 • *Learn more about all the major league teams*

MINOR LEAGUE BASEBALL   www.minorleaguebaseball.com
 • *Learn more about the minor leagues*

ON THE BOOKSHELF

To learn more about the sport of baseball, look for these books at your library or bookstore:

 • Kelly, James. *Baseball*. New York, New York: DK, 2005.

 • Jacobs, Greg. *The Everything Kids' Baseball Book*. Cincinnati, Ohio: Adams Media Corporation, 2006.

 • Stewart, Mark and Kennedy, Mike. *Long Ball: The Legend and Lore of the Home Run*. Minneapolis, Minnesota: Millbrook Press, 2006.

Index

The Team

MARK STEWART has written more than 25 books on baseball, and over 100 sports books for kids. He grew up in New York City during the 1960s rooting for the Yankees and Mets, and now takes his two daughters, Mariah and Rachel, to the same ballparks. Mark comes from a family of writers. His grandfather was Sunday Editor of the *New York Times* and his mother was Articles Editor of *Ladies' Home Journal* and *McCall's*. Mark has profiled hundreds of athletes over the last 20 years. He has also written several books about his native New York and New Jersey, his home today. Mark is a graduate of Duke University, with a degree in history. He lives with his daughters and wife, Sarah, overlooking Sandy Hook, NJ.

JAMES L. GATES, JR. has served as Library Director at the National Baseball Hall of Fame since 1995. He had previously served in academic libraries for almost fifteen years. He holds degrees from Belmont Abbey College, the University of Notre Dame, and Indiana University. During his career Jim has authored several academic articles and has served in an editorial capacity on multiple book, magazine, and museum publications, and he also serves as host for the Annual Cooperstown Symposium on Baseball and American Culture. He is an ardent Baltimore Orioles fan and enjoys watching baseball with his wife and two children.